All rights Reserved. No part of this publication or the information in it may be quoted from or reproduced in any form by means such as printing, scanning, photocopying or otherwise without prior written permission of the copyright holder.

Disclaimer and Terms of Use: Effort has been made to ensure that the information in this book is accurate and complete, however, the author and the publisher do not warrant the accuracy of the information, text and graphics contained within the book due to the rapidly changing nature of science, research, known and unknown facts and internet. The Author and the publisher do not hold any responsibility for errors, omissions or contrary interpretation of the subject matter herein. This book is presented solely for motivational and informational purposes only.

Presented by French Number Publishing
French Number Publishing is an independent publishing house headquartered in Paris, France with offices in North America, Europe, and Asia.
FN⁰ is committed to connecting the most promising writers to readers from all around the world. Together we aim to explore the most challenging issues on a large variety of topics that are of interest to the modern society.

SOUS VIDE CLASSICS

COOKING AT HOME

By Victor Ragnarson

FREE DOWNLOAD

YOUR FREE GIFT!
GET MORE FREE RECIPES IN 1 CLICK!

SIGN UP HERE TO GET YOUR
FREE SOUS VIDE SNACKS AND DESSERTS RECIPES
www.frenchnumber.net/sousvide

TABLE OF CONTENTS

Sous vide –so good! Cooking under vacuum the french way for delicious recipes and results................... 8

Cutting edge technology with french culinary roots . . . 8

The many advantages of cooking sous vide 9

Sous vide meets the home cook...................... 10

The versatility of sous vide 13

Home sous vide tips and tricks...................... 13

The first rule of sous vide is safety 16

BREAKFAST

POACHED EGGS 22

CREAMY BUTTERNUT SQUASH CASSEROLE 24

CHEESY MUSHROOM EGG WHITES 26

CLASSIC BUTTERNUT SQUASH WITH BUTTER....... 28

MOIST CARROT CAKE 30

BROWN SWEET POTATOES 32

CREAMY TOMATO EGGS........................... 34

DELICIOUS CORN CEREAL 36

STEAMED SPICED CAULIFLOWER 38

BAKED POTATO CASSEROLE 40

JUICY SOUS VIDE CHICKEN 42

BANANA ALMOND BREAD 44

ZUCCHINI CASSEROLE 46

SPECIAL BROWN RICE WITH CURRANTS............. 48

SOFT FRENCH TOAST 50

TABLE OF CONTENTS

LUNCH

FRESH MINT ASPARAGUS 54

GARLIC CHICKEN WITH BROCCOLI 56

DELICIOUS BOK CHOY IN LIGHT GRAVY 58

SIMPLE SHRIMP SALAD 60

REFRESHING SWEET CHICORY 62

TUNA VEGGIE FRITTER 64

CREAMY BUTTERNUT WITH SWEET CASHEW 66

DELICIOUS CHICKEN SALAD IN TOMATO SAUCE 68

COCONUT BROWN BEEF 70

BALSAMIC CABBAGE WITH CURRANTS 72

BUTTERNUT SQUASH SALAD 74

SIMPLE CHICKEN SALAD 76

TUNA LEMON SALAD 78

GARLIC CHICKEN WITH SWEET SOY SAUCE 80

ENERGIZING GOLDEN BEETS 82

DINNER

SWEET CHICKEN WITH FRESH BASIL 88

SWEET SOY BEEF RIBS 90

WARM BEEF SOUP WITH GINGER 92

HONEY GLAZED SHRIMP WITH PINEAPPLE 94

SWEET BROWN TURKEY 96

TROPICAL GRILLED DUCK LEGS 98

BLACK PEPPER PORK WITH CABBAGE 100

SIMPLE SALTY SEA BASS 102

SIMPLE BLACK PEPPER CHICKEN 104

SCRUMPTIOUS BLACK SQUID 106

CRISPY BROWN DUCK 108

SPICED FRIED CHICKEN THIGHS 110

MOIST SHRIMP IN RED SAUCE 112

CONCLUSION 114

Sous Vide –So Good! Cooking under vacuum the French way for delicious recipes and results.

Sous Vide, (pronounced soo veed), means under vacuum in French, and is a method of cooking where ingredients are vacuum sealed in a plastic bag and then placed in a water or steam bath, and cooked for long periods of time at low heat, producing food that is evenly cooked through without overcooking the outside. This results in moist, succulent, aromatic food, regardless of the shape or thickness of the raw ingredients. This unique cooking technique allows cooks of all calibers to make delicious meals, including meats that are tender, moist and flavorful and vegetables that retain their original firm texture while being fully cooked and pasteurized.

Cutting Edge Technology With French Culinary Roots

Food has been cooked in sealed packages throughout culinary history. Whether wrapped in leaves, folded into parchment or sealed inside animal bladders, it has long been a well-known secret shared by cooks, that food that is packaged in some manner before cooking preserves it and keeps it from drying out.

In the 1970s, French food researchers and chefs were looking for a technique to improve product yield while preserving the quality of foie gras, a classic French delicacy made of duck or goose liver. They discovered that when they cooked the liver in vacuum sealed plastic in a water bath for an extended period of time at a much lower temperature, their product yield soared without sacrificing quality. The process of sous vide cookery was born and the trend in professional kitchens and 5 star restaurants across the globe began to increase exponentially, as chefs realized sous vide could be used to produce and preserve haut cuisine of all types and specialties.

The Many Advantages of Cooking Sous Vide

Besides ensuring that the world will never be without a steady supply of foie gras (which, in itself is a worthy cause!), there are many more advantages of cooking sous vide:

- Tasty, appealing, economical food: the process of cooking sous vide guarantees zero dehydration of ingredients and preserves original size, form, color, and flavor. This technique also breaks down tough fibers in cheaper cuts of meat, transforming them into tender, delicious sources of protein.

- A healthier alternative: because the sous vide process literally "seals" in flavor, aroma and natural juices, there is little need for additional fat or salt. Along, with flavor and aroma, sous vide also locks in vitamins and minerals that are sometimes lost using other cooking methods.

- Consistent results: because the temperature can be controlled so precisely when cooking sous vide, it ensures consistent quality when preparing favorite foods and meals.

- Eliminates "burnt offerings": often, in an attempt to ensure that food has cooked completely through, reaching an ideal core temperature, the results can end up unappealing and overcooked.

- Helps coordinate cooking time: because food can be prepared and sealed in advance, it can be cooked in a more coordinated manner with other menu items.

- Cooking large quantities: cooking sous vide allows many individual portions to be prepared in a consistent manner that ensures quality results.

Sous Vide Meets The Home Cook

So how does the technical culinary darling of celebrity chefs; a cutting edge cooking method featured in the movie, Burnt, starring Bradley Cooper, translate into the workaday world of home cooking? Until quite recently, the expensive equipment required for sous vide cookery prevented its availability to the general public as a viable cooking method. In 2009, however, the first home sous vide system became available. Costing $449, it was still, undeniably, a high-end home kitchen appliance, but infinitely less expensive than the 4 figure price tag of restaurant machines. Today there are many home sous vide machines available at $200 and under. The other good news is that they are incredibly easy to operate!

There are basically two types of commercially available sous vide home systems: sous vide ovens and immersion circulators. Sous vide ovens are an "all in one" sous vide system that includes the vessel or "water oven" that you cook the vacuumed packed food in. Immersion circulators are a new addition: an immersible element that can be used with any pot (or bucket!) of water, transforming it into sous vide oven. Sous vide ovens are similar in size to a slow cooker, while immersion circulators more closely resemble large immersion blenders, and can be conveniently stored in a kitchen drawer.

So what is the best way to seal your food when cooking sous vide at home? It is important to properly seal sous vide pouches to prevent food juices from leaching into the water bath, keep the bags from floating during the cooking process, prohibiting air from acting as a poor heat transmitter, and to store food both before the sous vide cooking process. Although highly effective, chambered vacuum sealers are among the most expensive, and due to their size and weight, unwieldy appliances on the home market. Edge sealers are a moderately priced and less bulky alternative and are also great for pre-packaging food for freezer storage. They are not as effective at sealing in liquids, however. Surprisingly, you can also use Ziploc freezer bags, which are economical and very effective at sealing in liquids! Ziploc are also great because you can unseal and reseal them during the cooking process to check in on meat tenderness, or if the bag starts to float during longer cooking processes. You can even use oven bags, mason jars, and ceramic ramekins.

Finally, it is possible to sous vide at home without a sous vide oven or immersion circulator. Basically, all you need is a vessel to use as a water bath, a digital thermometer, and Ziploc bags. The hardest part of the process is maintaining a consistent temperature on your stovetop long enough to complete the required sous vide processing time. This can be accomplished by adjusting the stove burner as well as where you position the water bath vessel over it. Here are the basic steps to stovetop sous vide:

- Fill a pot with water
- Attach digital thermometer to side of pot
- Heat water to temperature required by recipe
- Place food in Ziploc bag
- Cook for time required in recipe
- Sear, if meat dish and you desire blackened "crust."
- Season and plate!

The Versatility Of Sous Vide

Many people think sous vide is a great method of cooking meat and leave it at that. But sous vide is an alternative method for cooking many different types of food and beverages! Here are just a few that might surprise and/or inspire you:

Alcoholic and non-alcoholic infusions, shrubs and syrups – the sous vide process enhances natural flavors and low temps speed up the process. What could be better, or easier to make all those retro cocktails and sodas currently in fashion?

Homemade ricotta cheese, crème fraiche, and yoghurt – the ability to control temperature precisely results in perfect fresh ricotta, crème fraiche and yoghurt every time.

Sauces, Collis, condiments, and compotes – make your own all natural condiments, including mustard, ketchup, chutney and more. Makes fool-proof hollandaise sauce for perfect eggs benedict every time. Dress up desserts with homemade fruit coulis and compotes.

Pickled vegetables and infused vinegar and oils – make your favorite pickled vegetables and vinegar without any lingering odors!

Home Sous Vide Tips and Tricks

As with any cooking technique, there are definitely some good-to-know tips that will make your first sous vide experiences more positive and productive:

- Use a tight fitting lid for your sous vide "oven," with a cutout for immersion element if you are using one. This will prevent water evaporation during the cooking process. Water evaporation can cause unit damage and tamper with consistent heat needed for proper sous vide cooking process.

- Be careful in your selection of sous vide herbs and seasonings. Some herbs will overpower the flavor or even taste spoiled if left too long a time period in the sealed bag of ingredients. Dried herbs seem to work better than fresh in the sous vide process. If using fresh herbs or onion and/or garlic, temper or cut back on the amount you would usually use as too much of these flavorings will alter the taste of your dish.

- Check for air gaps between the sealed pouch and the food being prepared. Air gaps can result in uneven cooking.

- When using commercial sous vide oven, place on insulated material to protect the counter surface. Unless you are confident, your counter top is heat and water resistant, protect it from possible dis- coloration.

- Make sure your cooking pouch doesn't float or "bob" during cooking. This will result in inconsist- ent cooking. Make sure there are no air pockets in bag and weigh down light food with safe food weights.

- Pre-sear meats before the sous vide process. This will add amazing extra flavor to beef, pork, and game. Don't pre-sear fish or delicate meats.

- Place seared meat in a pouch and immerse in ice water bag to bring the temp down to 38 degrees F before proceeding with sous vide process. This will prevent food from boiling in the bag from being too hot from searing process.

- Freeze bags containing liquids for a few minutes before sealing. This will set the liquids and prevent moisture from effecting vacuum and/or sealing process.

- Don't cook foods for more time than the recipe says. Cooking for longer times will not improve the quality of the finished product. More, in this case, is not better!

When it comes to the correct temperature to properly cook in the sous vide style, they are generally much lower than what would be considered a normal cooking temp. However, cooking is subjective, and when it comes to issues of texture and/or crispness of firmness, checking as you cook will be your best bet. Because water is such a great, even heat conductor, you don't have to worry about uneven heating or the hot or cold spots that can occur when using conventional cooking methods and appliances. Basically, when you cook sous vide, you are cooking your food until the center reaches the perfect temperature of "doneness." However, if after this temperature has been reached and the food remains in the water bath, it simply cannot overcook as the temperature of the bath will never exceed the desired temperature of the cooked food.

In addition to adapting this flexible, creative and consistent cooking technique from professional chefs, we can also "borrow" their sous vide tricks to enhance the visual presentation of the finished sous vide product.

• Use Oil in the cooking pouch. Adding an ample amount of oil to cooking pouches before cooking will prevent food from warping and keep its edges sharp, instead of developing a white, gluey edge around the perimeter of poultry and fish.

• Slice food after the sous vide cooking process rather than prepping before. It's easier to slice cooked food more evenly and will prevent the food from looking dry or discolored.

• Lower the temperature to preserver color. When preparing vegetables, preserver their vibrant color by cooking at a slightly lower temperature.

• Clip pouches that hold eggs to the side of the pot when cooking. This will prevent the gelatinous, goopy part of the egg white from forming and will result in a perfectly cooked, uniformly textured egg.

The First Rule Of Sous Vide Is Safety

Up until a few years ago, unless you were a professionally trained chef, cooking in the sous vide method was strongly discouraged and even considered by some sources to be a dangerous practice. Thankfully with the advent of home sous vide systems, paired with much more readily available educational materials and a few universal precautions, this philosophy has changed. Probably the most important safety rule for the home sous vide cook, is to consume all food cooked by this method immediately and not to store sous vide food in the manner that restaurants and caterers do. There is a very good reason for this precaution. Professional cooks are carefully trained and certified in food safety courses specifically designed to ensure proper handling of cooked and stored sous vide food. This part of the process is very detailed and precise, and it is better to err on the side of caution than to risk food borne illness for you or anyone you care enough to cook for.

The other safety issue you have to keep in mind concerns the basic principle of sous vide cookery. This method of cooking involves sealing raw or partially cooked foods in plastic bags and submerging them in a carefully, and consistently controlled water bath for relatively long periods of time, using relatively low levels of heat. When done correctly, this cooking process slowly pasteurizes, or kills harmful bacteria, in the foods, including poultry and meats, making them safe to consume. You have to be vigilant about the temperature consistency throughout this process.

Some people are also concerned about cooking food in plastic. Bags sold specifically for sous vide cooking as well as most if not all plastic Ziploc type food storage freezer bags are free of the hormone-disrupting chemicals that have raised alerts in the past. If you still have concerns, you can purchase food grade silicone bags which are also reusable and more environmentally friendly.

Here are some additional specific tips to safe sous vide:

Follow universal safety and hygiene precautions when preparing food to be cooked in the sous vide method, as you would with any conventional cooking techniques.

- Make sure raw ingredients are fresh, high quality and thoroughly cleaned before use.
- Buy sushi grade fish when cooking sous vide fish dishes
- Do not cook whole chickens unless using a vacuum chamber. Air trapped in the body cavity will cause the bag to float, resulting in uneven cooking.
- Follow instructions precisely
- Always fill water bath with fresh water, and change between uses.
- Don't overfill bags or overload the bath with too many bags.
- Always ensure you complete the full cooking time required for the item
- Use suitable food probes to test the core temperature of the food you are cooking
- Make sure thermometer is digital and in working order every time you use it. Follow instructions on how to use a thermometer and how to attach it to the cooking vessel.

- Avoid sous vide cooking if you or someone you are cooking for is immunocompromised, or in fragile heath. This would include pregnant women, young children and the elderly.

SOUS VIDE

BREAKFAST

Breakfast

POACHED EGGS

SERVES — 2 / PREPARATION TIME — 2 MIN. / COOKING TIME — 60 MIN.

 ## INGREDIENTS

4 fresh eggs
Salt, as needed
Pepper, as needed

Nutrition per serving

CALORIES — 126   PROTEIN — 11.1   FIBER — 0
SUGARS — 0.7   FAT — 8.8

INSTRUCTIONS

1. Set the Sous Vide machine to 143 F and fill with water.

2. Once the machine reaches the targeted temperature, gently add the eggs into the water bath.

3. Cook the eggs for 60 MIN. and once they are done carefully remove the eggs from the Sous Vide machine.

4. Peel the eggs then enjoy with salt and pepper.

TIP

If you want to consume them later, the poached eggs can be stored in a refrigerator for up to 48 hours.

Breakfast

CREAMY BUTTERNUT SQUASH CASSEROLE

SERVES — 2 / PREPARATION TIME — 10 MIN. / COOKING TIME — 45 MIN.

 ## INGREDIENTS

1 cup	diced butternut squash
1 tbsp.	chopped onion
¼ cup	fresh milk
3	organic eggs
2 tbsp.	breadcrumbs
¼ tsp.	salt
¼ tsp.	pepper

Nutrition per serving

CALORIES — 170   PROTEIN — 11   FIBER — 1.9
SUGARS — 4.1   FAT — 7.6

INSTRUCTIONS

1. Set the Sous Vide machine to 183°F or 84°C then wait until the Sous Vide machine achieves the targeted temperature.

2. Place all ingredients in a bowl and mix until combined.

3. Divide the mixture into two jars, cover with lids and seal properly.

4. Place the jars in the water bath then cook for 45 minutes.

5. Once it is done, remove jars from the Sous Vide machine and transfer to a serving dish.

6. Best enjoyed within a day.

TIP

Carrots and parsnips are great substitutions that you can try for this recipe. Enjoy!

Breakfast

CHEESY MUSHROOM EGG WHITES

SERVES — 4 / PREPARATION TIME — 10 MIN. / COOKING TIME — 60 MIN.

 ## INGREDIENTS

8	organic egg whites
½ cup	chopped mushrooms
¼ tsp.	salt
¼ cup	chopped onion
¼ tsp.	garlic powder
1-½ tbsp.	water
¼ tsp.	pepper

Nutrition per serving

CALORIES — 80   PROTEIN — 15.2   FIBER — 0.6
SUGARS — 1.9   FAT — 0.3

INSTRUCTIONS

1. Prepare 4 jars with lids.

2. Set the Sous Vide machine to 170 °F or 75°C and wait until it reaches the targeted temperature.

3. Meanwhile, place the egg whites in a bowl and season with garlic powder, pepper, and salt. Mix until incorporated and smooth.

4. Add chopped mushrooms and onion into the egg mixture and stir well.

5. Divide the mixture evenly into the four jars then cover and vacuum seal properly.

6. Submerge the jars in the Sous Vide machine and cook for an hour.

7. Once done, remove jars from the Sous Vide machine and serve.

8. This dish will taste best if you consume it in an hour.

TIP

If you like spicy taste, you can add about 1 tablespoon of red chili flakes into the mixture before cooking.

Breakfast

CLASSIC BUTTERNUT SQUASH WITH BUTTER

SERVES — 4 / PREPARATION TIME — 5 MIN. / COOKING TIME — 60 MIN.

 ## INGREDIENTS

2 butternut squash
1 tbsp. butter
A pinch of salt
½ teaspoon pepper

Nutrition per serving

CALORIES — 58   PROTEIN — 0.8   FIBER — 1.5
SUGARS — 1.5   FAT — 3

INSTRUCTIONS

1. Peel the butternut squash and dice.

2. Place the diced butternut squash in a Sous Vide plastic bag and add butter.

3. Sprinkle salt and pepper over the butternut squash and vacuum seal the plastic bag properly.

4. Set the Sous Vide machine to 183°F or 84°C and wait until it reaches the desired temperature.

5. Place the plastic bag into water bath and cook for an hour.

6. Once done, take the plastic bag out of the Sous Vide machine and let rest for about 5 minutes.

7. Cut open plastic bag and transfer the cooked squash to a serving dish.

8. Serve and enjoy while warm.

TIP

Don't choose overripe butternut squash or it will be mushy. Some people love this with cinnamon. Give it a try!

Breakfast

MOIST CARROT CAKE

SERVES — 2 / PREPARATION TIME — 15 MIN. / COOKING TIME — 3 HOURS

 ## INGREDIENTS

½ cup	grated carrot
4 tbsp.	palm sugar
3 tbsp.	almond oil
1	organic egg
½ tsp.	lemon juice
½ cup	multipurpose flour
½ tsp.	cinnamon
¼ tsp.	salt
¼ tsp.	baking powder

Nutrition per serving

CALORIES — 198   PROTEIN — 6.1   FIBER — 6
SUGARS — 0.4   FAT — 7.3

INSTRUCTIONS

1. Set the Sous Vide machine to 190°F or 88°C then wait until the Sous Vide machine achieves the targeted temperature.

2. Prepare 2 medium jars and brush with cooking spray. Set aside.

3. Combine carrot with palm sugar, almond oil, egg, and lemon juice in a bowl then mix until combined.

4. Next, stir the multipurpose flour into the bowl with cinnamon, salt, and baking powder.

5. Divide the mixture into two jars then seal them properly.

6. Place the jars in the water bath then cook for 3 hours.

7. Once done, remove the jars from the Sous Vide machine and let them cool for a few minutes.

8. Serve and enjoy within a day.

Breakfast

BROWN SWEET POTATOES

SERVES — 2 / PREPARATION TIME — 10 MIN. / COOKING TIME — 45 MIN.

 ## INGREDIENTS

1 lb. sweet potatoes
1 tbsp.   brown sugar
2 tbsp.   butter

Nutrition per serving

CALORIES — 193   PROTEIN — 1.8   FIBER — 4.7
SUGARS — 2.8   FAT — 6

INSTRUCTIONS

1. Peel the sweet potatoes and cut into slices.

2. Place the sliced sweet potatoes in a Sous Vide plastic bag and add butter.

3. Vacuum seal the bag properly then set aside.

4. Set the Sous Vide machine to 183°F or 84°C then wait until the Sous Vide machine achieves the targeted temperature.

5. Place the plastic bag into the water bath and cook for 45 minutes.

6. Once done, remove the bag from the Sous Vide machine and transfer to a serving platter.

7. Sprinkle brown sugar over the sweet potatoes and serve.

8. Best enjoyed within 6 hours.

TIP

Sprinkle grated cheese over the sweet potatoes for a savory twist.

Breakfast

CREAMY TOMATO EGGS

SERVES — 4 / PREPARATION TIME — 5 MIN. / COOKING TIME — 30 MIN.

 ## INGREDIENTS

4 large eggs
1 cup   heavy cream
½ cup   cherry tomatoes
Salt, as needed
1 tsp.   olive oil
¼ tsp.   black pepper

Nutrition per serving

CALORIES — 189   PROTEIN — 7.1   FIBER — 0.3
SUGARS — 1   FAT — 17.3

INSTRUCTIONS

1. Fill the Sous Vide water oven with water then preheat to 160°F or 71°C.

2. Crack the eggs then place in a blender.

3. Add the heavy cream into the blender then season with salt. Blend until incorporated.

4. Pour the egg mixture evenly into 4 mason jars then close the lids properly.

5. Place in the preheated Sous Vide water oven and cook for 25 minutes.

6. Meanwhile, make the topping:

7. Cut the cherry tomatoes into halves then combine with olive oil and black pepper. Mix well.

8. Once the eggs are done, remove from the Sous Vide water oven and top with the tomato mixture.

9. Serve and enjoy!

TIP

You can also have this egg plain. It will taste delicious on its own. Fresh strawberries with maple syrup also work well for this recipe.

Breakfast

DELICIOUS CORN CEREAL

SERVES — 2 / PREPARATION TIME — 10 MIN. / COOKING TIME — 30 MIN.

 ## INGREDIENTS

1 cup	corn kernels
2 tbsp.	butter
1 tbsp.	garlic powder
3 tbsp.	condensed milk
3 tbsp.	grated cheese

Nutrition per serving

CALORIES — 158   PROTEIN — 4.1   FIBER — 1.3
SUGARS — 9.6   FAT — 9.2

INSTRUCTIONS

1. Set the Sous Vide machine to 183°F or 84°C then wait until the Sous Vide machine achieves the targeted temperature.

2. Place the corn in a Sous Vide plastic bag then add butter and garlic powder. Vacuum seal bag properly.

3. Place the plastic bag in the water bath then cook for 30 minutes.

4. Once it is done, remove from the Sous Vide machine and transfer to a serving dish.

5. Drizzle condensed milk over the corn then sprinkle grated cheese on top.

6. Serve and enjoy within the hour.

Breakfast

STEAMED SPICED CAULIFLOWER

SERVES — 4 / PREPARATION TIME — 10 MIN. / COOKING TIME — 60 MIN.

 ## INGREDIENTS

2 cups cauliflower florets
2 tbsp. butter
1 tsp. minced garlic
1 tsp. sliced shallot
¼ tsp. pepper
¼ tsp. salt
1 tsp. fish sauce
1 cup fresh basil
½ cup coconut milk
Banana leaves, to wrap

Nutrition per serving

CALORIES — 163   PROTEIN — 2.4   FIBER — 2.8
SUGARS — 5.9   FAT — 13.1

INSTRUCTIONS

1. Place the cauliflower florets in a Sous Vide plastic bag.

2. Add butter into the plastic bag then vacuum seal.

3. Set the Sous Vide machine to 183°F or 84°C.

4. Once it reaches the targeted temperature, add the plastic bag into the water bath and cook for 45 minutes.

5. When the cauliflower is done, take the plastic bag out of the water bath and let it sit for a few minutes.

6. Cut open the plastic bag then transfer the cauliflower, without the liquid to a food processor. Process until consistency of grains of rice.

7. Combine the cauliflower "rice" with minced garlic, sliced shallot, pepper, salt, fish sauce, fresh basil, and coconut milk. Mix well.

8. Place 2 sheets of banana leaves on a flat surface then drop spiced cauliflower rice on each banana leaf.

9. Wrap the rice with banana leaves and shape into logs.

10. Place the wrapped cauliflower rice in a steamer over medium heat and steam for about 15 minutes.

11. Transfer to a serving dish and serve.

12. Best enjoyed within 4 hours.

TIP

A few red pepper flakes can be added to the cauliflower to give a little spicy kick. Enjoy!

Breakfast

BAKED POTATO CASSEROLE

SERVES — 2 / PREPARATION TIME — 10 MIN. / COOKING TIME — 90 MIN.

 ## INGREDIENTS

1 lb.	baby potatoes
1 tsp.	thyme
1 tsp.	garlic powder
¼ tsp.	salt
1 tbsp.	olive oil
3	organic eggs
½ cup	fresh milk
¼ cup	chopped onion
¼ cup	grated cheese

Nutrition per serving

CALORIES — 198   PROTEIN — 6.1   FIBER — 6
SUGARS — 0.4   FAT — 7.3

INSTRUCTIONS

1. Set the Sous Vide machine to 183°F or 84°C then wait until the Sous Vide machine achieves the targeted temperature.

2. Meanwhile, peel and cut baby potatoes into slices and place in a Sous Vide plastic bag. You don't need to peel them.

3. Season with thyme, garlic, and salt then splash olive oil over the potatoes.

4. Vacuum seal the bag properly then place in the Sous Vide machine. Set the timer for an hour and 15 MIN. and cook.

5. Once done, take the bag out of the Sous Vide machine and transfer to a casserole dish.

6. Mix egg and milk in a bowl and mix until incorporated.

7. Pour the mixture over the potatoes and sprinkle chopped onion and grated cheese on top.

8. Preheat an oven to 350°F, and bake the casserole until the eggs are set.

9. Once done, remove the casserole from the oven and serve.

10. Enjoy immediately since it is best served hot or warm.

Breakfast

JUICY SOUS VIDE CHICKEN

SERVES — 2 / PREPARATION TIME — 5 MIN. / COOKING TIME — 60 MIN.

 ## INGREDIENTS

1 lb. boneless chicken breast
¼ tsp.   salt
1 tsp.   olive oil
1 tbsp. butter
1 tsp.   cornstarch
2 tbsp. water

Nutrition per serving

CALORIES — 253   PROTEIN — 32.8   FIBER — 0
SUGARS — 0   FAT — 5

INSTRUCTIONS

1. Set the Sous Vide machine to 146°F or 63°C then wait until the Sous Vide machine achieves the targeted temperature.

2. Cut the chicken into thick slices and place in a Sous Vide bag.

3. Sprinkle salt over the chicken and add butter.

4. Vacuum seal the plastic bag and place in the water bath.

5. Sous Vide cook for 60 MIN. then remove from the Sous Vide machine.

6. Preheat a saucepan over medium heat and pour olive oil into it.

7. Stir in the chicken then sauté until brown. Transfer to a serving dish.

8. Pour the liquid into the skillet then pour the cornstarch and water mixture into the saucepan.

9. Bring to a simmer and stir until the liquid is thickened.

10. Drizzle the liquid over the chicken.

11. Best consumed in an hour.

TIP

Choose the boneless chicken breast without skin to avoid consuming too much fat.

Breakfast

BANANA ALMOND BREAD

SERVES — 6 / PREPARATION TIME — 20 MIN. / COOKING TIME — 2 HOURS

 ## INGREDIENTS

2 cups	mashed banana
¾ cup	almond flour
½ tbsp.	cinnamon
1 tsp.	baking powder
¼ cup	almond oil
½ cup	palm sugar
½ tsp.	salt
2	organic eggs

Nutrition per serving

CALORIES — 233 PROTEIN — 5.4 FIBER — 3.1
SUGARS — 8 FAT — 17.7

INSTRUCTIONS

1. Set the Sous Vide machine to 195°F or 90.5°C then wait until the Sous Vide machine achieves the targeted temperature.

2. Prepare 2 medium jars and brush with cooking spray. Set aside.

3. Combine almond flour with cinnamon and baking powder in a mixing bowl. Mix well.

4. In another bowl, place mashed banana, palm sugar, almond oil, eggs, and salt and mix until incorporated.

5. Pour the liquid mixture into the dry mixture then whisk until combined.

6. Divide the batter into six jars then cover with lids.

7. Place the jars in the water bath and cook for 2 hours.

8. Once done, take the jars out of the Sous Vide machine and let them cool for a few minutes.

9. Serve and enjoy within 24 hours.

Breakfast

ZUCCHINI CASSEROLE

SERVES — 2 / PREPARATION TIME — 10 MIN. / COOKING TIME — 45 MIN.

 ## INGREDIENTS

¾ lb.	sliced zucchini
¼ cup	chopped onion
1 tbsp.	butter
¼ tsp.	salt
¼ tsp.	black pepper
¼ cup	fresh milk
1	organic egg
2 tbsp.	chopped celery

Nutrition per serving

CALORIES — 132   PROTEIN — 6.1   FIBER — 2.4
SUGARS — 5.2   FAT — 8.9

INSTRUCTIONS

1. Set the Sous Vide machine to 183°F or 84°C then wait until the Sous Vide machine achieves the targeted temperature.

2. Combine all ingredients except chopped celery and mix well.

3. Transfer to a Sous Vide plastic bag then vacuum seal it properly.

4. Place the plastic bag in the water bath and cook for 45 minutes.

5. Once done, remove bag from the Sous Vide machine then transfer to a serving dish.

6. Sprinkle chopped celery on top and enjoy within a day.

Breakfast

SPECIAL BROWN RICE WITH CURRANTS

SERVES — 4 / PREPARATION TIME — 10 MIN. / COOKING TIME — 3 HOURS

 ## INGREDIENTS

½ tbsp.	olive oil
2 tbsp.	chopped leek
1 tsp.	minced garlic
¼ tsp.	salt
½ cup	uncooked brown rice
2 tbsp.	currants
1 cup	low sodium chicken broth
2 tbsp.	toasted chopped walnuts

Nutrition per serving

CALORIES — 267   PROTEIN — 6.7   FIBER — 2.6
SUGARS — 0.8   FAT — 9.4

INSTRUCTIONS

1. Preheat a skillet over medium heat and pour olive oil in it.

2. Once hot, stir in minced garlic, and salt then sauté until combined.

3. Add currants and rice into the skillet and stir until the rice is completely seasoned.

4. Remove the rice from heat and transfer to a Sous Vide plastic bag.

5. Pour chicken broth into the plastic bag then vacuum seal the plastic bag.

6. Set the Sous Vide machine to 180°F or 82°C.

7. Once it reaches the targeted temperature, add the plastic bag into the water bath and cook for 3 hours.

8. Once it is done, remove from the water bath then transfers the rice to a serving dish.

9. Enjoy while it is still warm or consume later (not more than 10 hours after cooking)

Breakfast

SOFT FRENCH TOAST

SERVES — 2 / PREPARATION TIME — 5 MIN. / COOKING TIME — 60 MIN.

 ## INGREDIENTS

2	slices bread
1	organic egg
4 tbsp.	heavy cream
½ tsp.	vanilla extract
¼ tsp.	cinnamon
2 tbsp.	butter

Nutrition per serving

CALORIES — 205   PROTEIN — 1.7   FIBER — 6.7
SUGARS — 16.8   FAT — 11.8

INSTRUCTIONS

1. Set the Sous Vide machine to 147°F or 64°C then wait until the Sous Vide machine achieves the targeted temperature.

2. Crack the egg and place in a bowl.

3. Combine the egg with heavy cream, vanilla extract, and cinnamon and mix until incorporated.

4. Dip each slice of bread into the mixture then place in a Sous Vide plastic bag.

5. Pour the remaining liquid mixture into the plastic bag and vacuum seal the plastic bag properly.

6. Place in the water bath then Sous Vide cook for 60 minutes.

7. Once it is done, remove the plastic bag from the Sous Vide machine then open it.

8. Preheat a saucepan over medium heat and add butter.

9. Once the butter is melted, put the bread in the saucepan and sear until both sides of the bread are brown.

10. Arrange on a serving dish and enjoy within an hour.

TIP

You can also put some extra topping on the finished bread to enrich the taste and beautify the appearance. Fruits, chocolate, or cheese will all work for this recipe.

SOUS VIDE

LUNCH

Lunch

FRESH MINT ASPARAGUS

SERVES — 2 / PREPARATION TIME — 5 MIN. / COOKING TIME — 20 MIN.

 ## INGREDIENTS

2 handfuls trimmed asparagus
¼ cup   butter
¼ tsp.   salt
1 tbsp.   chopped mint leaves

Nutrition per serving

CALORIES — 232   PROTEIN — 3.3   FIBER — 3
SUGARS — 2.5   FAT — 23.2

INSTRUCTIONS

1. Set the Sous Vide machine to 185°F or 85°C then wait until the Sous Vide machine achieves the targeted temperature.

2. Place trimmed asparagus in a Sous Vide plastic bag and add butter.

3. Sprinkle salt over the asparagus and vacuum seal the plastic bag properly.

4. Place in the water bath then Sous Vide cook for 20 minutes.

5. Remove the plastic bag from the Sous Vide machine then open the plastic bag.

6. Transfer the asparagus to a serving dish then drizzle the cooking liquid over it.

7. Sprinkle chopped mint leaves on top then serve.

8. Best to be consumed within an hour since cold asparagus does not taste as good as when warm.

TIP

You can also enjoy this asparagus with a pork chop. This is a great side dish for pork.

Lunch

GARLIC CHICKEN WITH BROCCOLI

SERVES — 4 / PREPARATION TIME — 5 MIN. / COOKING TIME — 70 MIN.

 ## INGREDIENTS

1 lb. chopped chicken
1 tbsp. butter
1 tsp. garlic powder
1 tsp. olive oil
1 tsp. minced garlic
1-cup broccoli florets
¼ tsp. pepper

Nutrition per serving

CALORIES — 218   PROTEIN — 33.7   FIBER — 0.7
SUGARS — 0.6   FAT — 7.6

INSTRUCTIONS

1. Set the Sous Vide machine to 146°F or 63°C then wait until the Sous Vide machine achieves the targeted temperature.

2. Rub the chicken with garlic powder then place in a Sous Vide plastic bag.

3. Add butter into the plastic bag and vacuum seal it properly.

4. Place the sealed plastic bag into the water bath and cook for 60 minutes.

5. Once it is done, remove from the Sous Vide machine.

6. Preheat a saucepan over medium heat then pour olive oil into it.

7. Stir in minced garlic then sauté until brown and aromatic.

8. Add broccoli into the saucepan then stir and cook until just wilted.

9. After that, open the plastic bag and add the chicken into the saucepan to warm.

10. Stir well then transfer to a serving dish.

11. Best to be enjoyed in 30 MIN. while it is warm. Especially for the broccoli, do not eat it after 8 hours. Any vegetables with high iron (the green vegetables) should be eaten immediately (not more than 8 hours after cooking).

TIP

This dish is best enjoyed within 30 MIN. when it is warm and the broccoli is still crunchy. However, it is ok to eat it a few hours later.

Lunch

DELICIOUS BOK CHOY IN LIGHT GRAVY

SERVES — 2 / PREPARATION TIME — 5 MIN. / COOKING TIME — 20 MIN.

 INGREDIENTS

1 lb.	chopped Bok Choy
1 tbsp.	ginger
1 tsp.	minced garlic
1 tbsp.	canola oil
1 tbsp.	low sodium soy sauce
1 tbsp.	fish sauce
1 tbsp.	sesame seed
1 tbsp.	cilantro
½ tsp.	salt

Nutrition per serving

CALORIES — 137   PROTEIN — 5.5   FIBER — 3.3
SUGARS — 3.3   FAT — 9.9

INSTRUCTIONS

1. Preheat a saucepan then pour canola oil into the saucepan.

2. Place the minced garlic and ginger in a bowl then pour the heated oil over the spices. Mix well.

3. Next, stir in soy sauce, fish sauce, and chopped Bok Choy, mix then transfer to a Sous Vide plastic bag and seal properly. Set aside.

4. Set the Sous Vide machine to 183°F or 84°C.

5. Once it reaches the targeted temperature, add the plastic bag into the water bath and cook for 20 minutes.

6. When done, take the plastic bag out from the water bath and open it.

7. Transfer to a serving dish then add salt. Stir well.

8. Garnish with sesame seeds and cilantro then enjoys within 6 hours.

TIP

Add the salt at the last minute before serving to keep the Bok Choy green.

Lunch

SIMPLE SHRIMP SALAD

SERVES — 2 / PREPARATION TIME — 5 MIN. / COOKING TIME — 30 MIN.

 ## INGREDIENTS

¾ lb.	shrimp
¼ tsp.	salt
1 tsp.	olive oil
1 tsp.	garlic powder
1 tbsp.	chopped parsley

Nutrition per serving

CALORIES — 114   PROTEIN — 19.5   FIBER — 0.1
SUGARS — 0.2   FAT — 2.6

INSTRUCTIONS

1. Set the Sous Vide machine to 140°F or 60°C then wait until the Sous Vide machine achieves the targeted temperature.

2. Peel and devein the shrimp then place in a Sous Vide plastic bag.

3. Add the remaining ingredients into the bag then vacuum seal it properly.

4. Place in the water bath and Sous Vide cook for 30 minutes.

5. Once it is done, remove the plastic bag from the Sous Vide machine and open the plastic bag.

6. Transfer the shrimp to a serving dish along with the cooking liquid.

7. Best enjoyed within an hour.

Lunch

REFRESHING SWEET CHICORY

SERVES — 2 / PREPARATION TIME — 5 MIN. / COOKING TIME — 20 MIN.

 ## INGREDIENTS

1 lb.	chicory
1 cup	unsweetened orange juice
¼ teaspoon	ginger
1 tsp.	honey
¼ tsp.	salt
¼ tsp.	pepper

Nutrition per serving

CALORIES — 117   PROTEIN — 4.7   FIBER — 9.4
SUGARS — 9.5   FAT — 0.9

INSTRUCTIONS

1. Cut the outer leaves off the chicory then place the rest in a Sous Vide plastic bag.

2. Season the chicory with ginger, salt, and pepper and pour orange juice and honey over the chicory.

3. Vacuum seal the plastic bag properly then set aside.

4. Set the Sous Vide machine to 183°F or 84°C then wait until the Sous Vide machine achieves the targeted temperature.

5. Once it reaches the desired temperature, place the plastic bag into the water bath and cook for 20 minutes.

6. When the Chicory is done, remove from the Sous Vide machine and transfer to a serving dish.

7. Enjoy within 12 hours.

TIP

Add about a tablespoon of red chili flakes if you like a spicy taste.

Lunch

TUNA VEGGIE FRITTER

SERVES — 2 / PREPARATION TIME — 5 MIN. / COOKING TIME — 45 MIN.

 ## INGREDIENTS

½ lb.	tuna chunks
1	organic egg
4 tbsp.	chopped onion
4 tbsp.	chopped leek
3 tbsp.	breadcrumbs
2 tbsp.	coconut milk
¼ tsp.	salt
¼ tsp.	garlic powder
¼ tsp.	black pepper

Nutrition per serving

CALORIES — 242   PROTEIN — 30.8   FIBER — 1.5
SUGARS — 2.7   FAT — 7.4

INSTRUCTIONS

1. Place all ingredients in a bowl then mix until combined.

2. Shape the mixture into medium patties then arrange in a container.

3. Put the container in a freezer and let it sit for about 2 hours or until the patties are firm.

4. Set the Sous Vide machine to 126°F or 52°C then wait until the Sous Vide machine achieves the targeted temperature.

5. Remove the patties from the freezer then transfer them to a Sous Vide plastic bag.

6. Vacuum seal the plastic bag then place in the water bath.

7. Sous Vide cook for 30 MIN. then remove from the Sous Vide machine.

8. Preheat a saucepan over medium heat then coat with cooking spray.

9. Sear the patties in the saucepan then transfer to a serving dish.

10. Best consumed within 6 hours.

TIP

Salmon and other kinds of fish will also work for this recipe. Add chopped mushrooms into the fritter for variety.

Lunch

CREAMY BUTTERNUT WITH SWEET CASHEW

SERVES — 4 / PREPARATION TIME — 5 MIN. / COOKING TIME — 30 MIN.

 ## INGREDIENTS

1 cup	cashews
1 tbsp.	olive oil
1 tsp.	cinnamon
1 tsp.	brown sugar
2 cups	chopped butternut squash
½ tsp.	sugar
2 tbsp.	lemon juice
1-cup	low sodium vegetable broth

Nutrition per serving

CALORIES — 270 PROTEIN — 6 FIBER — 2.8
SUGARS — 4.9 FAT — 19.5

INSTRUCTIONS

1. Preheat an oven to 400 °F or 204 °C then line a baking sheet with aluminum foil. Set aside.

2. Pour olive oil into a bowl then adds cashews.

3. Sprinkle cinnamon and brown sugar over the cashews and mix well.

4. Transfer the coated cashews to the prepared baking sheet and spread evenly in a single layer.

5. Bake until the cashews are lightly golden and crispy.

6. Remove from the oven and set aside.

7. Next, set the Sous Vide machine to 183°F or 84°C then wait until the Sous Vide machine achieves the targeted temperature.

8. Place the butternut squash in a Sous Vide plastic bag then add minced garlic and lemon juice.

9. Vacuum seal the plastic bag properly then place in the water bath.

10. Sous Vide cook for 30 MIN. then remove from the Sous Vide machine.

11. Cut the plastic bag then transfer the butternut squash to a blender along with the cooking liquid.

12. Blend until smooth then pour into a soup bowl.

13. Sprinkle sweet cashews over the soup and enjoy within an hour.

Lunch

DELICIOUS CHICKEN SALAD IN TOMATO SAUCE

SERVES — 4 / PREPARATION TIME — 15 MIN. / COOKING TIME — 70 MIN.

 ## INGREDIENTS

1 lb.	boneless chicken
1 tbsp.	butter
1 tsp.	garlic powder
¼ tsp.	pepper
1 tsp.	olive oil
2 tbsp.	chopped onion
1-cup	cherry tomatoes
1 tbsp.	tomato paste
¼ tsp.	sugar
¼ tsp.	salt

Nutrition per serving

CALORIES — 268   PROTEIN — 33.6   FIBER — 0.9
SUGARS — 2.3   FAT — 12.6

INSTRUCTIONS

1. Rub the chicken with garlic powder and pepper then let it sit for about 10 minutes.

2. Set the Sous Vide machine to 146°F or 63°C then wait until the Sous Vide machine achieves the targeted temperature.

3. Place the seasoned chicken in a Sous Vide plastic bag then add butter. Vacuum seal it properly.

4. Place the sealed plastic bag into the water bath and cook for 60 minutes.

5. Once it is done, removes from the Sous Vide machine.

6. Preheat a saucepan over medium heat then pour olive oil into it.

7. Stir in chopped onion then sauté until wilted and aromatic.

8. Cut the cherry tomatoes into halves then stir into the saucepan.

9. Add tomato paste then stir in the chicken together with the liquid.

10. Bring to a simmer then season with salt and sugar.

11. Transfer to a serving dish and enjoy warm.

12. Best to be enjoyed in 30 minutes.

TIP

If you don't like tomatoes, you can substitute them with chopped pineapple. Stir in the pineapple at the last minute.

Lunch

COCONUT BROWN BEEF

SERVES — 5 / PREPARATION TIME — 10 MIN. / COOKING TIME — 4 HOURS

 ## INGREDIENTS

1 lb.	chopped beef
¼ tsp.	salt
½ tsp.	pepper
1 tsp.	garlic powder
½ tsp.	thyme
¼ cup	butter
2 tbsp.	vegetable oil
1 cup	grated coconut
2 tbsp.	brown sugar
1	lemon grass
½ tsp.	coriander
¼ tsp.	ginger

Nutrition per serving

CALORIES — 233   PROTEIN — 17.7   FIBER — 1
SUGARS — 2.9   FAT — 16

INSTRUCTIONS

1. Season the beef with salt, pepper, garlic powder, and thyme and place in a Sous Vide plastic bag. Set aside.

2. Set the Sous Vide machine to 135°F or 66°C then wait until the Sous Vide machine achieves the targeted temperature.

3. Add butter into the plastic bag, vacuum seal and place in the water bath.

4. Sous Vide cook for 4 hours then remove from the Sous Vide machine.

5. Preheat a saucepan over low heat and add olive oil.

6. Once it is hot, stir in grated coconut then season with lemon grass, coriander, ginger and brown sugar.

7. Stir and cook the grated coconut until brown then add the beef without the liquid. Mix well.

8. Transfer to a serving dish and enjoy immediately.

TIP

If you want to eat it later, store in a container with a tight lid then consume within half a day.

Lunch

BALSAMIC CABBAGE WITH CURRANTS

SERVES — 1 / PREPARATION TIME — 5 MIN. / COOKING TIME — 20 MIN.

 ## INGREDIENTS

¾ lb. chopped red cabbage
2 tbsp. currants
1 tsp. sliced shallots
1 tsp. minced garlic
1-½ tsp. balsamic vinegar
1 tsp. butter
¼ tsp. salt

Nutrition per serving

CALORIES — 134   PROTEIN — 4.9   FIBER — 9.2
SUGARS — 12   FAT — 4.2

72

INSTRUCTIONS

1. Set the Sous Vide machine to 183°F or 84°C then wait until the Sous Vide machine achieves the targeted temperature.

2. Place the chopped red cabbage in a Sous Vide plastic bag.

3. Sprinkle shallot, garlic, and currants over the cabbage and add butter.

4. Vacuum seal the plastic bag and place in the water bath.

5. Cook the cabbage for 20 MIN. and once it is done, remove from the Sous Vide machine.

6. Open the plastic bag then transfer the cooked cabbage to a serving dish.

7. Season with salt and balsamic vinegar and stir until mixed.

8. Best enjoyed within two hours.

Lunch

BUTTERNUT SQUASH SALAD

SERVES — 4 / PREPARATION TIME — 10 MIN. / COOKING TIME — 45 MIN.

 ## INGREDIENTS

1 lb.	butternut squash cubes
1 tbsp.	diced sage leaves
½ tsp.	cinnamon
½ tsp.	ground cloves
3 tsp.	butter
¼ tsp.	salt
¼ tsp.	pepper
4 tbsp.	chopped walnuts
4 tbsp.	goat cheese
1 tbsp.	maple syrup

Nutrition per serving

CALORIES — 271 PROTEIN — 12 FIBER — 3.7
SUGARS — 6.4 FAT — 17.7

INSTRUCTIONS

1. Set the Sous Vide machine to 183°F or 84°C then wait until the Sous Vide machine achieves the targeted temperature.

2. Place the diced butternut squash in a Sous Vide plastic bag then add diced sage, cloves, butter, salt, pepper, and cinnamon.

3. Vacuum seal the plastic bag properly then place in the water bath.

4. Sous Vide cook for 45 MIN. and once it is done, remove the plastic bag from the Sous Vide machine and open the plastic bag.

5. Transfer the butternut squash to a serving dish then top with goat cheese.

6. Sprinkle chopped walnuts over the goat cheese then drizzle maple syrup on top.

7. Serve and eat within a half-day to enjoy the best taste.

Lunch

SIMPLE CHICKEN SALAD

SERVES — 4 / PREPARATION TIME — 5 MIN. / COOKING TIME — 2 HOURS

 ## INGREDIENTS

1 lb. chicken breast, boneless
½ tsp.   salt
½ tsp.   pepper
1 tbsp.   garlic powder

Nutrition per serving

CALORIES — 223   PROTEIN — 33.2   FIBER — 0.3
SUGARS — 0.5   FAT — 8.4

INSTRUCTIONS

1. Set the Sous Vide machine to 150°F or 65°C then wait until the Sous Vide machine achieves the targeted temperature.

2. Wash and drain the chicken breast then season with salt, pepper, and garlic powder until the chicken is completely seasoned.

3. Place in the Sous Vide plastic bag then vacuum seal the plastic bag and place in the water bath.

4. Sous Vide cook for an hour for thin chicken or 2 hours for thicker chicken then remove from the Sous Vide machine.

5. Once it is done, remove from the water bath, plate and enjoy within 2 hours.

TIP

If you have varied thicknesses of chicken, use the thickest pieces to determine the cooking time.

Lunch

TUNA LEMON SALAD

SERVES — 2 / PREPARATION TIME — 5 MIN. / COOKING TIME — 30 MIN.

 ## INGREDIENTS

1 cup	tuna chunks
1 tbsp.	olive oil
¼ tsp.	salt
1 tsp.	lemon zest
2 tbsp.	lemon juice

Nutrition per serving

CALORIES — 124   PROTEIN — 13.1   FIBER — 0.1
SUGARS — 0.4   FAT — 7.6

INSTRUCTIONS

8. Set the Sous Vide machine to 140°F or 60°C then wait until the Sous Vide machine achieves the targeted temperature.

9. Place tuna chunks in a Sous Vide plastic bag then add olive oil, salt, lemon zest, and lemon juice.

10. Vacuum seal the plastic bag properly then place in the water bath and Sous Vide cook for 30 minutes.

11. Once it is done, remove the plastic bag from the Sous Vide machine and open it.

12. Transfer the tuna chunks to a serving dish together with the liquid.

13. Best enjoyed within an hour.

Lunch

GARLIC CHICKEN WITH SWEET SOY SAUCE

SERVES — 4 / PREPARATION TIME — 10 MIN. / COOKING TIME — 3 HOURS

 ## INGREDIENTS

½ lb. boneless chicken breast
¼ cup   butter
1 tsp.   dried basil
Salt, as needed
½ tsp.   pepper
2 tsp.   minced garlic
2 tbsp.   sweet soy sauce

Nutrition per serving

CALORIES — 371   PROTEIN — 17.3   FIBER — 0.2
SUGARS — 0.2   FAT — 15.7

INSTRUCTIONS

1. Fill the Sous Vide water oven with water then preheat to 146 °F or 63°C.

2. Place the chicken breast in a Sous Vide plastic bag then add a tablespoon of garlic, butter, pepper, salt, and basil.

3. Vacuum seal the bag properly then submerge in the water bath and cook for 3 hours.

4. Once it is done, take it out from the water bath and cut the plastic.

5. Pour the liquid into a saucepan then bring to a simmer over low heat.

6. Stir in the remaining garlic then add the chicken into it.

7. Sear until golden then transfer to a serving dish.

8. Drizzle sweet soy sauce on top then serve.

9. Enjoy!

TIP

Choose an organic chicken for the most tasteful dish.
Sprinkle sesame seeds on top to beautify the appearance and enhance the flavor.

Lunch

ENERGIZING GOLDEN BEETS

SERVES — 4 / PREPARATION TIME — 5 MIN. / COOKING TIME — 90 MIN.

 ## INGREDIENTS

1 lb. golden beets
1 cup unsweetened orange juice
¼ cup lemon juice
¼ cup butter
1 tbsp. honey
1 tsp. black pepper
1 tsp. salt

Nutrition per serving

CALORIES — 199 PROTEIN — 2.7 FIBER — 2.3
SUGARS — 19.2 FAT — 11.7

INSTRUCTIONS

1. Set the Sous Vide machine to 183°F or 84°C then wait until the Sous Vide machine achieves the targeted temperature.

2. Cut the beets into thick slices then place in a Sous Vide plastic bag together with the remaining ingredients.

3. Vacuum seal the plastic bag properly then place in the water bath and Sous Vide cook for 90 minutes.

4. Once it is done, remove the plastic bag from the Sous Vide machine and open the plastic bag.

5. Pour the beets and the liquid into a saucepan and bring to a simmer until the liquid has reduced by half.

6. Transfer to a serving dish and enjoy immediately.

½ lb. chicken fillet

SOUS VIDE

DINNER

Dinner

KALE SOUP WITH ROASTED CHICKPEAS

SERVES — 4 / PREPARATION TIME — 5 MIN. / COOKING TIME — 30 MIN.

 ## INGREDIENTS

1 cup	chickpeas
1 tbsp.	olive oil
1 tsp.	paprika
1 tsp.	cayenne powder
2 cups	chopped kale
1 tsp.	minced garlic
2 tbsp.	lemon juice
1 cup	low sodium vegetable broth
1 cup	chopped onion
1 tsp.	vegetable oil

Nutrition per serving

CALORIES — 260   PROTEIN — 11.2   FIBER — 10.2
SUGARS — 7.1   FAT — 7.9

INSTRUCTIONS

1. Preheat an oven to 400 °F or 204°C then line a baking sheet with aluminum foil. Set aside.

2. Pour olive oil into a bowl then add chickpeas to it.

3. Sprinkle paprika and cayenne over the chickpeas and mix well.

4. Transfer the chickpeas to the prepared baking sheet and spread evenly in a single layer.

5. Bake until the chickpeas are completely golden and crispy.

6. Remove from the oven and set aside.

7. Next, set the Sous Vide machine to 183°F or 84°C then wait until the Sous Vide machine achieves the targeted temperature.

8. Place the chopped kale in a Sous Vide plastic bag then add minced garlic and lemon juice to it.

9. Vacuum seal the plastic bag properly then place in the water bath.

10. Sous Vide cook for 30 MIN. then remove from the Sous Vide machine.

11. Cut the plastic bag then transfer the kale to a blender along with the cooking liquid.

12. Preheat a saucepan over medium heat then pour vegetable oil in it.

13. Once oil is hot, stir in chopped onion then sauté until wilted and aromatic.

14. Transfer the onion to the blender then blend all together until smooth.

15. Pour the kale soup into a soup bowl then sprinkle roasted chickpeas on top.

16. Serve and enjoy immediately.

TIP

This kale soup is best enjoyed immediately. Make sure to cook only enough for a one-time mealtime.

Dinner

SWEET CHICKEN WITH FRESH BASIL

SERVES — 4 / PREPARATION TIME — 10 MIN. / COOKING TIME — 4 HOURS

 ## INGREDIENTS

1 lb.	chopped chicken, bone in
1 stalk	lemon grass
1 bay	leaf
1 tsp.	olive oil
1 tbsp.	minced garlic
1 tbsp.	sliced shallots
2 tbsp.	red chili flakes
1 tsp.	pepper
½ tsp.	salt
1 cup	fresh basil

Nutrition per serving

CALORIES — 195   PROTEIN — 33.5   FIBER — 0.5
SUGARS — 0   FAT — 4.7

INSTRUCTIONS

1. Set the Sous Vide machine to 150°F or 66°C then wait until the Sous Vide machine achieves the targeted temperature.

2. Place chopped beef in a Sous Vide plastic bag then add lemon grass and bay leaf.

3. Vacuum seal it properly then add the plastic bag into the water bath

4. Cook for 4 hours and once it is done, remove from the Sous Vide machine then let it sit for a few minutes.

5. Next, preheat a skillet over medium heat then pour olive oil into it.

6. Once it is hot, stir in minced garlic, sliced shallot and red chili flakes then sauté until golden and aromatic.

7. Add the Sous Vide beef into the skillet together with the cooking liquid then add fresh basil into the skillet.

8. Season with pepper and salt then bring to a simmer.

9. Transfer to a serving dish then enjoy within a half-day.

TIP

This dish is best served with a plate of warm rice. Enjoy!

Dinner

SWEET SOY BEEF RIBS

SERVES — 8 / PREPARATION TIME — 10 MIN. / COOKING TIME — 5 HOURS

 ## INGREDIENTS

2 lbs.	chopped beef ribs
1 tsp.	salt
1 tsp.	garlic powder
¼ tsp.	ginger
¼ tsp.	nutmeg
½ cup	soy sauce
½ tsp.	pepper

Nutrition per serving

CALORIES — 221   PROTEIN — 35.3   FIBER — 0.2
SUGARS — 0.4   FAT — 7.1

INSTRUCTIONS

1. Set the Sous Vide machine to 140°F or 60°C then wait until it reaches the targeted temperature.

2. Rub the chopped ribs with salt, garlic powder, ginger, and nutmeg then place them in a Sous Vide plastic bag.

3. Vacuum seal the plastic bag then cook for 5 hours.

4. When the beef ribs are done, remove from Sous Vide machine then open the plastic bag.

5. Pour the liquid into a bowl and add soy sauce and pepper. Mix until incorporated.

6. Dip the beef ribs into the liquid mixture then let them sit for a few minutes.

7. Meanwhile, preheat a grill over medium heat and once it is done, grill the beef ribs until brown.

8. Transfer to a serving dish then enjoys while the ribs are hot (not more than 1 hour) for the best taste.

TIP

Sprinkle fried sliced shallots over the beef ribs. It will not only give extra delicacy and tempting aroma, but it also a crunchy texture.

Dinner

WARM BEEF SOUP WITH GINGER

SERVES — 8 / PREPARATION TIME — 15 MIN. / COOKING TIME — 4 HOURS

 ## INGREDIENTS

2 lbs.	chopped beef
¼ cup	chopped onion
½ cup	chopped celery
¼ tsp.	pepper
½ tsp.	nutmeg
½ tsp.	ginger
2 quarts water	

Nutrition per serving

CALORIES — 214   PROTEIN — 34.5   FIBER — 0.2
SUGARS — 0.3   FAT — 7.1

INSTRUCTIONS

1. Preheat an oven to 450°F or 232°C then line a baking sheet with parchment paper. Set aside.

2. Place the beef in a bowl together with chopped onion, celery, pepper, nutmeg, and ginger. Mix well.

3. Place all on the prepared baking sheet and bake for about 10 minutes.

4. Meanwhile, set the Sous Vide machine to 145°F or 63°C and wait until it reaches the targeted temperature.

5. Next, remove the beef from the oven and transfer all to a big Sous Vide plastic bag.

6. Pour water into the bag then seal it properly and cook for 4 hours.

7. Once it is done, transfer to a serving bowl and enjoy immediately.

TIP

This soup is best enjoyed immediately.

Dinner

HONEY GLAZED SHRIMP WITH PINEAPPLE

SERVES — 4 / PREPARATION TIME — 5 MIN. / COOKING TIME — 30 MIN.

 ## INGREDIENTS

¾ lb.	shrimp
¼ tsp.	salt
1 tsp.	olive oil
1 tsp.	garlic powder
1 tbsp.	butter
2 tbsp.	pineapple juice
¾ cup	pineapple chunks
2 tbsp.	honey

Nutrition per serving

CALORIES — 190   PROTEIN — 19.8   FIBER — 0.5
SUGARS — 12.6   FAT — 5.6

INSTRUCTIONS

1. Set the Sous Vide machine to 140°F or 60°C then wait until the Sous Vide machine achieves the targeted temperature.

2. Peel and devein the shrimp then place in a Sous Vide plastic bag.

3. Add the remaining ingredients into the bag and vacuum seal it properly.

4. Place in the water bath and Sous Vide cook for 30 minutes.

5. Once done, remove the plastic bag from the Sous Vide machine then open the plastic bag.

6. Preheat a saucepan on medium heat and add butter.

7. Once the butter is melted, stir in pineapple chunks then pour pineapple juice in. Stir well.

8. Add the shrimp into the saucepan then drizzle honey over the shrimp. Mix until combined.

9. Transfer to a serving dish and enjoy immediately.

Dinner

SWEET BROWN TURKEY

SERVES — 4 / PREPARATION TIME — 8 MIN. / COOKING TIME — 4 HOURS

 ## INGREDIENTS

2 lb. turkey thighs
2 tbsp.   lemon juice
¼ cup   butter
Salt, as needed
¼ cup   sweet soy sauce
1 tbsp.   palm sugar
½ tsp.   pepper

Nutrition per serving

CALORIES — 188   PROTEIN — 12.9   FIBER — 0.2
SUGARS — 1.4   FAT — 14.1

INSTRUCTIONS

1. Fill the Sous Vide water oven with water then preheat to 150°F or 66°C.

2. Place the turkey thighs in a Sous Vide plastic bag then add a tablespoon of butter, salt, sweet soy sauce, pepper, and palm sugar.

3. Vacuum seal the bag properly then submerge in the water bath and cook for 5 hours.

4. Once it is done, take it out of the water bath and cut the plastic.

5. Pour the liquid into a saucepan then bring to a simmer over medium heat.

6. Stir in the turkey thighs then sauté until the turkey thighs are brown.

7. Transfer to a serving dish then enjoy the dish while it is still warm.

Dinner

TROPICAL GRILLED DUCK LEGS

SERVES — 4 / PREPARATION TIME — 5 MIN. / COOKING TIME — 16 HOURS

 ## INGREDIENTS

1 lb.	duck legs
1 tbsp.	lemon juice
1 tsp.	lemon zest
½ tsp.	salt
¼ tsp.	sugar
1 tbsp.	butter
2 tbsp.	chopped mint leaves
¾ cup	chopped pineapple

Nutrition per serving

CALORIES — 246   PROTEIN — 33.3   FIBER — 3.3
SUGARS — 3.4   FAT — 9.7

INSTRUCTIONS

1. Set the Sous Vide machine to 165°F or 74°C. Wait until it reaches the targeted temperature.

2. Place the duck legs in a Sous Vide plastic bag then add lemon zest, sugar, and salt.

3. Pour lemon juice over the duck legs then vacuum seal the plastic bag.

4. Place the plastic bag into the water bath and cook for 16 hours.

5. Once it is done, remove from the Sous Vide machine then open the plastic bag.

6. Preheat a grill over medium heat then brush the duck legs with butter.

7. Grill the duck legs until brown then transfer to a serving dish.

8. Sprinkle mint leaves and chopped pineapple on top then serve.

9. Enjoy while the duck is hot (not more than 1 hour later) for the best taste.

Dinner

BLACK PEPPER PORK WITH CABBAGE

SERVES — 4 / PREPARATION TIME — 15 MIN. / COOKING TIME — 24 HOURS

 ## INGREDIENTS

1 lb.	pork shoulder
1 tsp.	salt
½ tsp.	black pepper
1 tsp.	olive oil
1 cup	chopped cabbage
1 tbsp.	lemon juice
1 tsp.	Dijon mustard
2 tbsp.	mayonnaise
2 tbsp.	avocado oil

Nutrition per serving

CALORIES — 386   PROTEIN — 28.9   FIBER — 9.7
SUGARS — 1.1   FAT — 28.9

INSTRUCTIONS

1. Set the Sous Vide machine to 160°F or 71°C then wait until the Sous Vide machine achieves the targeted temperature.

2. Sprinkle salt and pepper on the pork shoulder then place in a Sous Vide plastic bag.

3. Vacuum seal the plastic bag then place in the water bath.

4. Cook the pork shoulder, setting the timer for 24 hours.

5. The next day, combine chopped cabbage with lemon juice, Dijon mustard, mayonnaise, and avocado oil. Stir well then set aside.

6. Next, preheat a cast iron skillet over medium heat then pour olive oil into it.

7. Pat dry the cooked pork shoulder then sear in the cast iron skillet until brown.

8. Flip the pork and do the same to the other side.

9. Place the pork on a platter then serve with the cabbage.

10. Best to be enjoyed within an hour. Enjoying it warm is best since the pork is still tender.

Dinner

SIMPLE SALTY SEA BASS

SERVES — 2 / PREPARATION TIME — 5 MIN. / COOKING TIME — 30 MIN.

 ## INGREDIENTS

½ lb. fresh sea bass
¾ tbsp. olive oil
¼ tsp.   salt

Nutrition per serving

CALORIES — 296   PROTEIN — 30   FIBER — 1.6
SUGARS — 0.8   FAT — 10.8

INSTRUCTIONS

1. Set the Sous Vide machine to 126°F or 52°C then wait until the Sous Vide machine achieves the targeted temperature.

2. Brush the sea bass with olive oil then season with salt.

3. Place the seasoned sea bass in a plastic bag then vacuum seal the plastic bag properly.

4. Place the plastic bag in the water bath and Sous Vide cooks for 30 minutes.

5. Once it is done, remove the plastic bag from the Sous Vide machine then let it sit for an hour. Open the plastic bag.

6. Transfer to a serving dish then enjoy within a maximum of 6 hours.

Dinner

SIMPLE BLACK PEPPER CHICKEN

SERVES — 4 / PREPARATION TIME — 10 MIN. / COOKING TIME — 3 HOURS

 ## INGREDIENTS

2 lb.	boneless chicken breast
¼ cup	butter
1 tsp.	dried basil
Salt, as needed	
½ tsp.	pepper
2 tbsp.	minced garlic
2 tbsp.	sweet soy sauce

Nutrition per serving

CALORIES — 221   PROTEIN — 17.3   FIBER — 0.2
SUGARS — 0.2   FAT — 15.7

INSTRUCTIONS

1. Fill the Sous Vide water oven with water then preheat to 146 °F or 64°C.

2. Place the chicken breast in a Sous Vide plastic bag then add a tablespoon of garlic, butter, pepper, salt, and basil.

3. Vacuum seal the bag properly then submerge in the water bath and cook for 3 hours.

4. Once it is done, take it out of the water bath and cut the plastic.

5. Pour the cooking liquid into a saucepan then bring to a simmer over low heat.

6. Stir in the remaining garlic then add the chicken into it.

7. Sear until golden then transfer to a serving dish.

8. Drizzle sweet soy sauce on top then serve.

9. Enjoy this delicious dish!

Dinner

SCRUMPTIOUS BLACK SQUID

SERVES — 2 / PREPARATION TIME — 5 MIN. / COOKING TIME — 2 hours

 ## INGREDIENTS

1 lb. fresh squid
¼ tsp.   salt
½ tsp.   coriander
1 tbsp.   olive oil
1 tbsp.   minced garlic
1 bay leaf

Nutrition per serving

CALORIES — 276   PROTEIN — 35.6   FIBER — 0.2
SUGARS — 0   FAT — 10.2

INSTRUCTIONS

1. Set the Sous Vide machine to 136°F or 58°C then wait until the Sous Vide machine achieves the targeted temperature.

2. Season the squid with all of the remaining ingredients then place in a Sous Vide plastic bag and seal properly.

3. Place in the water bath then Sous Vide cook for 2 hours.

4. Once it is done, remove from the Sous Vide machine and open the plastic bag.

5. Transfer to a serving dish then serve.

6. Best to be enjoyed within a couple of hours.

TIP

Do not discard the ink of the squid because it will enhance the taste, aroma, and the color of the dish.

Dinner

CRISPY BROWN DUCK

SERVES — 4 / PREPARATION TIME — 15 MIN. / COOKING TIME — 90 MIN.

 ## INGREDIENTS

1 lb. duck breast
¼ tsp. salt
½ tsp. black pepper
1 tsp. thyme
2 cloves garlic

Nutrition per serving

CALORIES — 150 PROTEIN — 25.1 FIBER — 0.2
SUGARS — 0 FAT — 4.6

INSTRUCTIONS

1. Set the Sous Vide machine to 140°F or 60°C then wait until the Sous Vide machine achieves the targeted temperature.

2. Place the duck breast in a Sous Vide plastic bag then add the remaining spices.

3. Place the plastic bag in the water bath then Sous Vide cook for 90 minutes.

4. Once it is done, remove the plastic bag from the Sous Vide machine and removes the duck from the plastic bag. Pat dry using a paper towel.

5. Preheat a saucepan over medium heat then brush with cooking spray.

6. Lay the duck on the saucepan then cook for about 30 seconds.

7. Flip the duck then cook again until both sides are brown.

8. Transfer to a serving dish and enjoy while warm.

Dinner

SPICED FRIED CHICKEN THIGHS

SERVES — 4 / PREPARATION TIME — 5 MIN. / COOKING TIME — 6 HOURS

 ## INGREDIENTS

1 lb.   chicken thighs
1 tsp.   garlic powder
½ tsp.   coriander
1 bay   leaf
2 kaffir lime leaves
½ tsp.   salt
1 lemon grass
¼ tsp.   turmeric
Vegetable oil, to fry

Nutrition per serving

CALORIES — 225   PROTEIN — 33   FIBER — 0.1
SUGARS — 0.2   FAT — 8.5

110

INSTRUCTIONS

1. Set the Sous Vide machine to 165°F or 74°C. Wait until it reaches the targeted temperature.

2. Place the chicken in a plastic bag then add garlic powder, coriander, bay leaf, kaffir lime leaves, lemon grass, turmeric, and salt.

3. Vacuum seal the plastic bag then place the plastic bag into the water bath and cook for 6 hours.

4. Once it is done, remove from the Sous Vide machine then open the plastic bag.

5. Preheat a frying pan over medium heat and pour vegetable oil in it.

6. Discard the chicken liquid then place the chicken thighs in the frying pan.

7. Fry the chicken until golden then flip and fry until both sides of the chicken are golden.

8. Transfer to a serving dish then enjoy not more than 10 hours later.

Dinner

MOIST SHRIMP IN RED SAUCE

SERVES — 4 / PREPARATION TIME — 5 MIN. / COOKING TIME — 30 MIN.

 ## INGREDIENTS

¾ lb. fresh shrimp
¼ tsp. salt
¼ tsp. baking soda
¼ cup olive oil
2 tbsp. sliced garlic
1 tbsp. smoked paprika
1 bay leaf
1 ½ tbsp. sherry
1 tsp. sherry vinegar
1 tbsp. butter

Nutrition per serving

CALORIES — 269 PROTEIN — 19.9 FIBER — 0.8
SUGARS — 0.2 FAT — 17.2

INSTRUCTIONS

1. Set the Sous Vide machine to 140°F or 60°C then wait until the Sous Vide machine achieves the targeted temperature.

2. Peel and devein the shrimp then rub with salt and baking soda and let sit for a few minutes.

3. Meanwhile, preheat a skillet over medium heat then pour olive oil into it.

4. Once it is hot, stir in sliced garlic then sauté until lightly brown and aromatic.

5. Add smoked paprika, bay leaf, sherry, and sherry vinegar then stir well. Set aside.

6. Place shrimp in a Sous Vide plastic bag then add butter and the oil mixture.

7. Vacuum seal the plastic bag properly then place in the water bath and Sous Vide cook for 30 minutes.

8. Once it is done, remove the plastic bag from the Sous Vide machine and open the plastic bag.

9. Transfer the shrimp to a serving dish and serve.

10. Best enjoyed within an hour.

TIP

The freshness of the shrimp determines the delicacy of this recipe. Choose the freshest shrimps you can find and avoid picking the shrimp that have display a pink hue.

Conclusion

I hope you have enjoyed reading about all of the delicious and versatile recipes in this cookbook. The sous vide cooking process is an exciting addition to any home cook's culinary repertoire and will add important tools to your menu options and meal preparations as well as enabling your finished creations to be fresh, healthy and aesthetically pleasing to the eye and the palate.

It is always an exciting moment when technology, economy and cutting edge cuisine align in a perfect storm, allowing home cooks to enjoy the delicious sophistication of restaurant quality food from the comfort of their own kitchens. Whether preparing a special meal for the family, a romantic dinner for two or a holiday celebration for friends far and near, the sous vide cooking process will elevate your chef and hosting skills to the next level. All it takes is a few streamlined appliances, the freshest, healthiest food available and a passion for fine cuisine paired with enthusiasm to learn new skills and understand the boundaries of the sous vide method — boundaries from within which your creativity and imagination for delicious food will soar!

Please use the recipes in this cookbook to learn all the different, delicious ways sous vide cooking can be incorporated into your daily life as well as allowing you to learn to transform inexpensive, tougher cuts of meat into tender gourmet dishes and something as simple as a humble poached egg into a thing of beauty, especially when served with a velvety helping of sous vide Hollandaise and and a few elegant toast points.

Bon Appetit!

FREE DOWNLOAD

YOUR FREE GIFT!
GET MORE FREE RECIPES IN 1 CLICK!

SIGN UP HERE TO GET YOUR
FREE SOUS VIDE SNACKS AND DESSERTS RECIPES
www.frenchnumber.net/sousvide

All information is intended only to help you cooperate with your doctor, in your efforts toward desirable weight levels and health. Only your doctor can determine what is right for you. In addition to regular check ups and medical supervision, from your doctor, before starting any other weight loss program, you should consult with your personal physician.

All rights Reserved. No part of this publication or the information in it may be quoted from or reproduced in any form by means such as printing, scanning, photocopying or otherwise without prior written permission of the copyright holder.

Disclaimer and Terms of Use: Effort has been made to ensure that the information in this book is accurate and complete, however, the author and the publisher do not warrant the accuracy of the information, text and graphics contained within the book due to the rapidly changing nature of science, research, known and unknown facts and internet. The Author and the publisher do not hold any responsibility for errors, omissions or contrary interpretation of the subject matter herein. This book is presented solely for motivational and informational purposes only.

Presented by French Number Publishing
French Number Publishing is an independent publishing house headquartered in Paris, France with offices in North America, Europe, and Asia.
FNº is committed to connecting the most promising writers to readers from all around the world. Together we aim to explore the most challenging issues on a large variety of topics that are of interest to the modern society.

Printed in Great Britain
by Amazon